Pens
& Writing Equipment
A Collector's Guide

Pens
& Writing Equipment

A Collector's Guide

Jim Marshall

MILLER'S PENS & WRITING EQUIPMENT: A COLLECTOR'S GUIDE
by Jim Marshall

First published in Great Britain in 1999 by Miller's, a division of
Mitchell Beazley, imprints of Octopus Publishing Group Ltd,
Michelin House, 81 Fulham Road, London SW3 6RB
First published in the USA in 1999
Copyright © Octopus Publishing Group Ltd
Miller's is a registered trademark of Octopus Publishing Group Ltd
This edition distributed in the USA by Antique Collectors' Club Ltd.,
Market Street Industrial Park, Wappingers' Falls, New York, NY 12590, USA

Executive Editor **Alison Starling**
Executive Art Editor **Vivienne Brar**
Project Editor **Elisabeth Faber**
Assistant Editor **Clare Peel**
Designers **Louise Griffiths & Adrian Morris**
Indexer **Sue Farr**
Production **Rachel Staveley**
Specially commissioned photography by **Tim Ridley**
Illustrations by **Stefan Chabluk** based on original drawings by **Jim Marshall**
Jacket photography by **Stuart Chorley**

ISBN 1 84000 146 1
A CIP catalog record for this book is available from the British Library
Set in Bembo, Frutiger, and Shannon
Color reproduction by Vimnice Printing Press Co. Ltd., Hong Kong
Produced by Toppan Printing Co., (HK) Ltd.
Printed and bound in China

Jacket (left to right): box of Waverley steel nibs by MacNiven & Cameron,
1935; ivory-and-silver seal by Mordan, 1890; sterling pencil, 1930; sterling
dip pen, 1900; grey geometric "Duofold" by Parker, 1934; portable "Swan"
ink bottle by Mabie Todd, 1930

contents

Where to start

For centuries writing has been a fundamental and reliable link between generations; it has facilitated communication across the world, been the means of broadcasting rules, regulations, and the organization of society, and acted as a vital medium for creative, religious, and literary pursuits. Much of our knowledge of the past is based on pictograms and the written word, whether in the form of hieroglyphics, clay tablets, parchment documents, or modern records on paper. When there are gaps in our knowledge of history, they invariably occur because no written documents exist to act as indicators of past events. However, although for the most part we now take the ability to write for granted, as a skill developed at school, it is only in the last 200 years that writing has been practiced by any more than a privileged few.

Before 1700 most writers in the western world were scribes, professional diarists, and those concerned with the law or with significant trades, or those educated by the church. Interestingly, while there are many examples of their labors (parchment documents, for example), the writing instruments and accessories used by early writers are extremely rare and seldom seen outside museums.

The most popular and collectible writing equipment originates from the end of the 18thC. At this time the demand for such items increased as a result of better education, the growth of overseas trade, colonization, and the general turbulence caused by the widespread agricultural and industrial reforms.

The 19thC was a period of great change, and many fine writing items were produced during that time. The transition from the use of the quill to the introduction of the steel nib, and then the production of the earliest fountain pens, provide great scope for collecting, as does the wide range of innovative mechanical pencils produced. Increased communication, the fashion for journals, diaries, and letter-writing, the introduction of the "penny" post, envelopes, and postcards, and the popularity of such desk accessories as inkstands and seals all mean that there is plenty of material from the 19thC to capture the collector's interest.

In the early 20thC fountain pens were firmly established as the most commonly used writing instruments and were widely promoted by modern marketing. Fountain pens maintained their position as market leaders until overtaken in the 1930s by new, more affordable innovations such as ballpoint pens, which are now becoming highly collectible in their own right.

Before 1980 there were few collectors of pens and writing equipment, and it is only in the last ten years that the enthusiasm of loyal writing-equipment devotees has stimulated the growth of clubs, societies, publications, and fairs to the point where these items form an

important feature of the antiques market. Fortunately, many writing items of different shapes, sizes, and styles produced since 1800 still survive, making it possible for a budding collector to find an absolute treasure at a sale, in an antiques market, or simply among forgotten effects in attics. Many such items can easily be repaired, restored and, most importantly, used.

This guide focuses on the range of popular writing collectables readily available at fairs and auctions, and in specialist shops. The most important factor when purchasing is always to buy what you like, not purely for investment; if you purchase items that you truly like, then by definition this is a good investment.

Major makers

This selection of makers (listed according to country of origin, although many are now fully international) may help when browsing through the markets.

American makers
Aiken Lambert
Chilton
Conklin Pen Co.
Eversharp Wahl
Fairchild
Parker
Salz
Sheaffer
Waterman

British makers
Burnham
Conway Stewart
De La Rue
Dunhill
Ford
Mabie Todd & Co.
MacNiven & Cameron Ltd
Mentmore
S. Mordan & Co.
Platinum
Stephens
Valentine & Co.
Wyvern Pen Co.

German makers
Haro
Montblanc
Pelikan

Italian makers
Omas
Visconti

Prices

Prices for antiques vary, depending particularly on the condition of the item, but also according to geographical location and market trends. The price ranges given throughout this book should be seen as a general indicator to value only.
Conversion rate: $1.65 = £1.00

Quills & early writing tools

Quills have been used for at least 13 centuries and were the most common form of writing instrument in the West until the end of the 19thC – the reed pen and brush were most popular in Asia. Geese were the most common source of quill, but feathers from swans, crows, turkeys, and ducks were also used. The finest quills were made from the first three flight feathers on each wing; after plucking, the tips were conditioned by being placed in hot ash, and the quills cut with a sharp knife. Both cut and uncut quills were sold by stationers and booksellers. Most scribes and clerks cut or sharpened their own quills, using a range of cutting tools, and quills were still used at the underwriters Lloyds of London until the 1980s.

▼ Parchment

Most early important documents, particularly deeds, were produced on parchment – the skin of an animal (usually a sheep or a goat). However, as paper improved in quality, parchment became much less widely used. Presentation was important, and scribes would pierce the sides of each page at regular intervals and join the holes with pencil lines, so that the text would be straight and neat.

▼ Boxes of quills

Most quills were trimmed to remove the barb and sold by the dozen. Quill slips (small quill nibs, popular from 1815 to 1840) were also sold by stationers. The boxes in which cut quills or quill slips were sold are rarely found in good condition but can be as valuable as the quills or slips themselves. Boxes of quill nibs by the firms of Bramah or Mordan are especially prized.

Left to right:
12 boxed quills,
1840, **$66–132**;
quill slips, 1825,
$82–132

Parchment
document, 1606,
$58–91; lead-
marker pencil, 1840,
$7–13

Left to right: eraser by Rodgers, 1840, **$33–49**; quill knife in a case, 1810, **$82–198**

▼ Pen-making tools

Commercial growth in the 19thC created an increasingly large number of written documents, which in turn boosted the writing-equipment business. In London most pen makers and stationers were located in Fleet Street, Cornhill, and Charing Cross. They specialized in selling quills and pen-making tools such as this rare early compendium, by Thomas Lund. With an ivory body and a lignum vitae case, it contains a wafer seal, wafers, quill-knife blades, a toothpick, and a lancet to stop the quill blades being used for bleeding.

Compendium by Lund, 1800, **$1,155–1,320**

▲ Writing tools

A scribe's main tools were a sharp knife and a spade-shaped "eraser" (such as the bone-handled example above) to scrape the parchment surface. The majority of tools were of horn, ebony, or ivory. Most very early knives have a peg on the end of a short stock, used to split the quill; later (19thC) knives have oval-shaped handles with pointed ends. From 1800 to 1900 small folding knives were used for cutting pens, and from c.1850 combined knives and erasers on one blade were popular. The value of a knife is increased if it is still with its original case (see the ivory quill knife above).

◀ Quill cutters

Although machines for cutting quills were first designed in the 17thC, the most common ones found today are those based on Bramah's patent of 1812. These hand machines, sold in morocco leather cases, had scissor-like mechanisms to form the quill and slit the nib. The handle, usually of ebony (right), ivory (far right), or horn, often had a folding or sliding knife blade and a device known as a "nibber", which could alter the slant or width of the nib.

Left to right: quill cutter, 1840, **$165–330**; quill cutter, 1850, **$247–412**

Early dip pens & nibs

The main disadvantage of quills and quill nibs was that they were soft and had to be frequently re-cut, which created a need for the invention of a more durable writing tool. Metal pens had been produced in the 18thC, but these early examples were either inflexible and easily corroded by the acid ink (those made of steel and brass) or too soft (those made of gold). With the development of flexible steel processing, the invention of coatings to reduce corrosion, and the use of less acidic inks, steel nibs gradually replaced quills. Birmingham in England became the center for the pen trade, and by 1880 more than one billion steel pen nibs were produced there every year.

◄ **Quill-slip and nib holders**
Dip pens require a clamping device or ferrel to secure the metal nib or quill slip. The early designs by Longmore and Bramah, shown left, used a complex slide-ring system, but were superseded by more economic simple ferrels from c.1845. The most common shafts are made of wood or metal, but some pens were produced in such exotic materials as mother-of-pearl, sharkskin, tortoiseshell, and porcupine quill.

Left to right: Longmore-design combination pen/pencil by Moseley, 1845, **$247–297**; sharkskin dip pen, c.1820, **$165–198**; porcupine pen with Bramah holder, c.1820, **$132–247**

▶ **Glass dip pens**
Dip pens made of glass were popular in the 19thC, but good examples are rare because fluted glass nibs were quite prone to chipping. Such pens were also sold as marking and copying pens because they could withstand heavy pressure. Colored examples and pens with figural finials are most prized. However, watch out for modern Italian reproductions.

Left to right: colored-glass pen, 19thC, **$82–132**; simple marking pen, 19thC, **$33–49**

▼ Steel nibs

A vast range of steel nibs for dip pens was produced in the 19thC for use in schools, offices, and banks, and by artists and calligraphers. The sample roll shown below would have been carried by a traveling salesman to present his range to prospective clients. This large example by A. Sommerville & Co. contains 440 different nibs of all different sizes and widths. As it was rarely clear whether a company had manufacturing facilities or purely subcontracted work, collectors of steel nibs generally refer to "issuers". Somerville was a founding partner of Perry & Co. and probably did not make nibs itself after 1870.

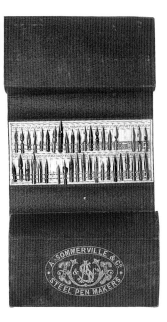

▼ Nib boxes

Many writing-equipment enthusiasts collect not only pens and nibs but also the boxes in which they were sold. The affordable examples illustrated below are just three of a vast range of different designs. Most Birmingham pen-making companies produced boxes of nibs for export, and packaged their products in a variety of designs and languages.

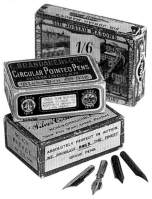

Top to bottom: box of nibs by Josiah Mason, 1845, **$16–20**; pen box by C. Brandauer, 1910, **$2–3**; box of silver-plated nibs made in Birmingham, 1920, **$2–3**

Nib roll by Sommerville, 1890, **$330–495**

Steel nibs
• It took between 12 and 15 stages of manufacture to produce steel nibs. The process involved: rolling and annealing Sheffield sheet steel; cutting and slitting the sides of nib blanks; further annealing; stamping and then curving the nib; tempering, grinding, and slitting the nib; and finally chemically treating and lacquering the end product.
• Despite this lengthy process, the large quantity produced kept prices low.

▼ Tubular nibs

Very early metal pens consisted simply of shaped tubes slipped over quills. The nib was integral to the tube (see below), which obviated the need for a ferrel. Such tubular nibs were often made for promotional purposes with custom-stamped logos, for example to advertise stationers' shops. Attractive boxes with one shaft and a dozen nibs are very collectible.

Tubular nibs, 1880, **$5–8** (each)

Later dip pens & stands

The dip pen was the most common writing instrument from 1840 until 1940, and they were still used in British schools (where traditional desks were fitted with porcelain inkwells) until the early 1950s. The variety from simple wooden-handled examples to exquisite, ornate designs is vast; some were made as individual items, others as part of writing sets for the desk or for travel. Pen stands, including those designed for communal writing areas in offices and banks, where dip pens were increasingly used to sign documents and checks, are becoming very collectible.

◀ Decorative dip pens

Many decorative dip pens were fashioned from silver and gold. Value is determined primarily by the quality of the decoration, the maker, the balance, and the quality and size of the nib. Pens with maker's marks, such as the silver example by the American Gorham Manufacturing Co. and the one by the British firm of Mordan shown here, fetch a premium, as do those with novelty mechanisms such as nib ejectors. Dents to the shaft and split nib holders (quite common) reduce the value.

▼ Pen stands

Stands and rests designed to hold a number of pens are often found as part of inkstands, but separate pen stands are rare. The example shown is made of cast iron, but similar ones were made in wood, brass, and silver. The two pens featured are a standard wooden dip pen and a popular mother-of-pearl retractable nib pen made by Mabie Todd in New York.

Pen stand, 1870, **$66–115**; dip pen, 1930, **$5–8**; dip pen by Mabie Todd, 1890, **$66–82**

Left to right: sterling silver spiral dip pen, 1900, **$82–132**; dip pen by Gorham, early 20thC, **$132–231**; hallmarked dip pen by Mordan, 1890, **$165–214**

Pen trays

Made in brass, pewter, glass, metal, and porcelain, pen trays are essentially desk tidiers designed to hold nibs, pens, and seals. Trays made of glass were often part of wooden inkstands. The example shown, in the form of a quill, is American; the engraved dip pen is made of ivory and silver.

Pen tray, 1900, **$165–247**; dip pen, 1890, **$99–132**

Notable designs

Other collectible dip pens include:

- crystal-shafted pens with filigree decoration (often of a small snake)
- agate-, amber-, or tortoiseshell-shafted pens (often sold in sets with a seal and a paper-knife)
- American sculptured pens by Unger Brothers (demand premium prices)
- examples with stanhopes in carved ivory, bog oak, or wood
- red, hard-rubber dip pens (Ormiston & Glass)
- Russian, French, and Italian multi-colored glass pens.

Left to right:
push-mechanism "combo", 1880, **$148–214**; twist-mechanism "combo", 1900, **$99–231**

◀ "Combos"

Many makers combined a dip pen and a pencil in one instrument, called a "combo". The two examples shown resemble dip pens, but other combinations are more compact and look like telescopic pencils. In the German example shown left, the pencil extends beyond the nib when the shaft is pushed; the American example works using a twist mechanism.

▼ Small pen stands

In addition to the large stands produced for use in offices and public-sector buildings, smaller stands for individual purposes were also made. The example shown is of cast bronze, but most were made in cast iron or brass. The dip pen is an unusual ebony design by Mabie Todd of New York and features a detachable gold tubular "No.7" nib – the larger the number, the bigger the nib.

Small pen stand, 1870, **$33–58**; dip pen by Mabie Todd, 1885, **$165–198**

Fountain pens: basics

When you purchase a pen, the two most important factors in determining its value are the condition and the originality. Dealers use a grading system to reflect the condition (*see* Fact File), which should help new enthusiasts; originality is best verified using a good reference manual (*see* pp.62–3). Experience will improve your judgment, but it is good practice to examine a prospective purchase carefully, using an eyeglass. It is quite probable that an 80-year-old pen will have been repaired, but if this has been carried out professionally, using the correct replacement parts, then the value should not be affected. There are three principal parts of a pen to check: the barrel (the main body of the pen and the filling system), the cap (including a clip or clip ring), and the nib unit (the nib and feed).

▼ **Caps and clips**
Caps, made from metal or plastic, often have another cap fitted internally to seal the pen, and either push or screw onto the barrel. Clips or ring tops are usually attached by rivets, lugs, or screws. Watch out for lip cracks, chips, shrinkage, discoloration, and broken clips, and make sure that the colors of the barrel and the cap match.

▶ **Barrels & filling systems**
The barrel is where the ink reservoir and filling system (usually involving a rubber sac or piston) are contained. When you examine a pen, never force the filling lever or piston as this may cause irreversible damage. Avoid examples with gaping lever slots, distorted barrels (check by rolling on a flat surface), cracks, cigarette burns, and bad discoloration, as most of these defects cannot be rectified.

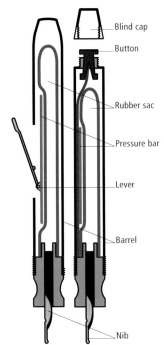

Blind cap

Button

Rubber sac

Pressure bar

Lever

Barrel

Nib

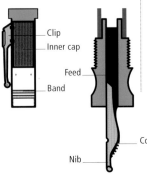

Clip
Inner cap
Feed
Band

Comb
Nib

▼ Components of a pen

The nib, which is normally 14- or 18-carat gold, should be in good condition, with an iridium tip. Check the name on the nib in case it is an inappropriate replacement, which would be costly to change; the section should not be damaged by tools, and the "comb" should not be broken. Old rubber sacs harden and disintegrate easily (see below), but this is not too great a problem, as they are simple to replace.

▼ Body materials

The first non-metal bodies were made of vulcanized rubber (usually black, reinforced with carbon; red, reinforced with iron oxide; or a mix of the two). From the 1920s plastics such as caesin and cellulose nitrate were used for barrels and caps in a variety of colors, patterns, and finishes (see below).

FACT FILE

Grading for condition

A: mint – never used, still in original wrapping.
B: excellent – as new.
C: very good – used, but everything present and in good working order.
D: good – some wear, scratches, slight brassing, complete with correct nib.
E: poor – scratches, brassing, unrepaired, bent nib.
F: valuable as parts only – some salvageable parts, not worth repair.

▼ Restoration

Pens that do not function are significantly less valuable than those in good working order. It is advisable, especially with very valuable pens, to leave repair to a professional restorer, as there is always a risk of damage, no matter how simple the repair. However, most pens can be restored to working condition, and restoration is becoming increasingly popular among collectors. Consequently, repair tools such as the Parker repair block, shown below center with J-shaped nib tool (below left) and black section clamp (below), are collectible as well as of practical use.

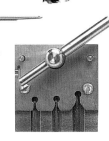

Fountain pens

A fountain pen is a pen that contains its own reservoir of ink. Such pens were mentioned *c.*1663 by the English diarist Samuel Pepys, and the earliest known examples were made *c.*1690 by Nicholas Bion, instrument maker to Louis XIV (reigned 1643–1715). Bion's pen design of a simple tubular metal reservoir leading to a quill nib was widely copied in the 18thC. During the 19thC, patents for reservoir pens were granted to an extensive range of manufacturers including Sheaffer, Parker, Folsch, and Moseley. However, many early pens suffered from irregular flow of ink to the writing tips, and an acknowledged breakthrough did not come until a feed system, which facilitated a regular supply of ink to the nib, was developed by the American firm of Waterman in 1883. This date is considered to be the birth of the fountain pen, and marks the start of the marketing of such pens.

◀ **Tapered caps**

Early fountain pens were made from tubes of ebonite with nib units screwed into them and caps to protect the nibs. Such pens were filled using bulbed rubber eyedroppers. Early examples featured protective "push-on" caps to protect the nibs, but such caps often cracked, so versions that tapered both in shape and internally were introduced. Caps did not feature pocket clips until c.1904. This pen (shown with its eyedropper) was made by Waterman; fountain pens made by this firm before 1900 are especially rare.

Pen by Waterman, c.1904,
$99–132

▶ **Cartridge pens**

The first popular cartridge pen was produced in the USA in the 1890s by the Eagle Pencil Co. of New York. A glass cartridge full of ink was pushed onto the peg of the nib unit and then fitted back into the barrel of the pen. Examples with spiral or black hexagonal cases are relatively rare but not of high value.

Cartridge pen, 1895,
$49–99

▼ Decorative pens
Pens with elaborately decorated cases have long been produced as symbols of wealth and status. Most decorative pens had bodies embellished with metal overlay, as black hard-rubber cases were considered dull. Many of these decorative pens were produced for pen companies by silversmiths, using such techniques as engraving, filigree, and repoussé. The rare and delicate silver pen featured below is by the firm of MacNiven & Cameron and features its trademark curved Waverly pen nib.

Pen with Waverly nib by MacNiven & Cameron, 1915, **$330–412**

▼ De-luxe designs
Some makers produced top-of-the-range fountain pens, decorated with exotic materials and heavily worked precious metals. Notable examples are by Heath for Parker (filigree and mother-of-pearl pens), and Waterman (elaborate silver designs). Such pens represent superb quality but are correspondingly highly priced. More affordable, and still very attractive, are the repoussé and gold-filled overlay pens of Mabie Todd, Aiken Lambert, Wirt, and Salz (shown left). American makers were particularly reputed for their overlay designs.

Fountain pen by Salz, 1910, **$115–165**

▶ Eyedroppers
Swan eyedroppers, made by Mabie Todd, were very successful and were made over a longer period (1895–1950) than any other eyedropper, making them the most common example found today. Early designs, such as the eyedropper hung from a châtelaine shown right, feature a bayonet cap, an under-and-over feed, and a twisted silver wire inside the barrel to improve the ink flow; later models used a single underfeed. Eyedroppers were also produced by Waterman over a fairly long period, and still featured in the firm's 1920s trade catalogs. Red-and-black vulcanite eyedroppers are quite rare and collectible.

Swan eyedropper by Mabie Todd, 1905, **$99–165**

Filling systems

From 1900 the main aim of pen makers was to produce self-filling pens that did not require any accessories (for example, eyedroppers). Most makers developed systems using flexible rubber sacs to hold the ink, and devised different ways of expelling air from the sac prior to filling, although some makers still used the barrel of the pen as the ink reservoir but with the addition of a piston or plunger. Both systems had their drawbacks – sacs perished, and piston seals deteriorated – but, in general, pens with rubber sacs were more practical than those without. Some enthusiasts concentrate solely on collecting pens that illustrate the range of filling systems invented; in addition to those shown, this includes blow fillers, coin fillers, matchstick fillers, and sleeve fillers.

◀ Piston fillers

The design for the piston filler used by the Onoto company, invented by George Sweester, was sold to Sir Evelyn De La Rue's firm in 1905. The two examples shown have early under-and-over feeds; the metal overfeed is part of a robust manifold nib and was designed for duplicating. De La Rue had made pens since 1881, but the piston model, which remained in production until the 1950s, was its most successful one. Gold and silver overlay models are particularly prized.

Left to right: piston pen by Onoto, 1910, **$82–132**; simple piston pen by Onoto, 1915, **$49–82**

▶ Crescent fillers

Conklin, originally based in Toledo, Ohio, is famous for its crescent filler, invented in 1898 and patented in 1901. A simple pressure bar fixed in position by a metal crescent and a rotating band was used to compress the rubber sac inside the barrel of the pen. This filling system helped to make Conklin the fifth largest pen company in the world by the 1920s.

Crescent filler with gold "Toledo No.3" nib by Conklin, c.1918, **$132–198**

▼ Piston fillers

Although the two pens shown below have pistons, they operate on very different principles. The "International" pen (left) features a simple suction syringe, which pulls ink into the barrel; the pen by Chilton (right) has a rubber sac with a piston system used to depress the sac. Pens by Chilton are of a high quality and very collectible. Pens with syringes have the disadvantage of a low-ink capacity.

Left to right: "International" pen, 1910, **$33–58**; pen by Chilton, 1925, **$99–132**

▶ Lever fillers

Although Sheaffer designed the lever filling system in 1907, it was not used until 1913 when the firm started production in Fort Madison. The filling system consisted of a lever fixed to the barrel, which adjusted a pressure bar to compress the rubber sac. Although far from perfect – the slot for fitting the lever often weakened or distorted the barrel, particularly with poor-quality plastic pens – the lever became the most popular and imitated filling system invented.

Lever filler by Sheaffer, 1916, **$82–132**

Company preferences
- In the 1920s major makers tended to use one filling system only:
  Eversharp Wahl: lever
  De La Rue: piston
  Parker: button
  Waterman: lever
  Sheaffer: lever
  "Swan": lever
- In the 1930s, all except Waterman used a variety of systems.

◀ Button fillers

Introduced c.1908, the button filler was adapted by Parker and used as its main filling system until the mid-1930s. The pressing down of a button covered by a blind cap caused the pressure bar to depress the rubber sac inside the pen. Button fillers were slightly more complicated to manufacture than lever fillers, but were more robust, and are among the easiest pens to repair. Examples were also made by Wyvern and Conway Stewart.

"Senior Duofold" by Parker, 1926, **$198–297**

Flat tops

From the earliest production of self-filling pens *c*.1905 until the late 1920s, the majority of fountain pens were designed as straight-sided tubes with flat tops and bottoms – hence the name "flat top". The earliest examples were produced in black hard rubber, then in red, and combinations of red and black. By the end of the 1920s all the major firms in Europe and the USA, including Mabie Todd, De La Rue, Parker, Waterman, Sheaffer, Eversharp Wahl, Bayard, Pelikan, and Omas, had moved from using hard rubber to production in the wide range of newly available, brightly colored synthetic polymers.

▶ New plastics

Sheaffer was the first company to use new materials on a large scale. In 1924 it introduced a new range of pens made from cellulose nitrate, which it called "Radite". These early Sheaffers were made in "black" and "coral" as well as "jade". These early pens tended to discolor and fade when exposed to light, or developed dark stains from coming into contact with ink. Examples with pristine color are rare and valuable, as color is probably the most important value factor for fountain pens.

"Radite" pen by Sheaffer, 1927, **$165–280**

◀ Rare designs

Pens that were difficult to manufacture, had performance weaknesses, or simply did not sell well, often had short production lives. As these pens were made only in small quantities they are now rare and often very collectible. The yellow "Mandarin Duofold" by Parker, produced from 1928 until 1932, is such an example and, although not a success with the public, is now one of the most sought-after pens among collectors. Unfortunately, the light color accentuates any defect in the body, so examples with good, clean, even color and no cracks in the cap command a premium.

"Mandarin Duofold Junior" by Parker, c.1930, **$412–577**

◀ Classic designs

The classic American-made Parker "Duofold" was introduced in 1922 and was an immediate success. Originally available in black or red hard rubber, it was produced from 1925 in "Permanite", and from 1926 in other colors, such as "lapis", "jade", and "pearl". The red version of the "Duofold Senior" became known as the "Big Red". The range included smaller and slimmer models such as the "Junior" (see left), the "Deluxe" with a broad cap band, and the rarest size, the "Special" (shown here), which is the same diameter as the "Junior" and the same length as the "Senior". Good "lapis", "pearl", and "jade" examples are rare; early examples, such as the red hard-rubber "Senior", which does not feature a cap band, are all highly priced.

"Duofold Special" by Parker, 1925, **$198–297**

▼ Woodgrain & mottled effects

Depending how black and other colors are extruded, mottled and woodgrain effects can be produced. Mabie Todd used mottled finishes, and Eversharp Wahl used woodgrain finishes for its red-and-black hard-rubber pens. The "Swan" flat-top lever fill shown is one of the largest models made. The "Personal Point" pen (also lever fill) by Eversharp Wahl has a unique roller-ball clip and a quality seal on the cap.

Left to right: "Swan" pen by Mabie Todd, 1926, **$412–577**; "Personal Point" by Eversharp Wahl, 1930, **$247–412**

FACT FILE

◀ Ripple effects

In 1929 the "94" pen by Waterman was available in "ripple rose", "ripple olive", and "ripple blue/green". Other Waterman ripples available, were in the "52" to "58" series or the "5" and "7" series. The "7" shown has a purple band on the cap and a keyhole nib, which is stamped "Purple" – Waterman's code for a stiff, fine-nibbed pen for shorthand and bookkeeping. Note the different positions of the clip on the cap.

Left to right: "ripple blue" by Waterman, 1929, **$198–264**; "ripple red 7" series by Waterman, 1927, **$247–330**

Innovations & desk units

In the 1920s and 1930s, as the fountain-pen market boomed, companies were continually trying to think of new ways to impress customers. Contrasts of different materials, overlays, dramatic use of color, metal trim, colored plastic rings, and colored grooves were all employed to increase a pen's attraction. Desk units – the successor to 19thC inkstands – became popular and were made in a dazzling range of shapes, sizes, and designs.

▼ **Mottled pens by Conway Stewart**

Early pens by Conway Stewart were lever-fill pens with stepped clips similar to those found on early "Swan" pens by Mabie Todd. Later 1930s models, as shown, featured ring clips and hard-rubber clip screws with integral inner caps. Black-and-red hard rubber was frequently used by Conway Stewart, not only for whole pens but also for sections and clip screws, thus adding elegant decoration to black barrels and caps.

Set by Conway Stewart, 1930s, **$115–198**

▲ **Filigree pens by Waterman**

Most pen manufacturers made premium products with overlay decoration to tempt customers (see pp.16–17). Overlay designs by Waterman, such as the example featured above, were very popular and were made in six versions – "Vine", "Filigree", "Gothic", "Sheraton", "Pansy", and "Basketweave" – in both silver or gold, and in a design known as "Moderne" in silver only. Good condition is vital with overlay designs, particularly on gold-filled examples, so check for lever damage and brassing.

"0552 Filigree" pen/pencil by Waterman, 1927, **$412–577**

▼ Color pens by Conklin

By the early 1920s the success of Conklin's crescent-fill pens (see pp.18–19) had established the firm's reputation as one of the leading American pen makers. The crescent filler was replaced by a simple lever filler c.1922. In general, ring tops such as the set shown below are less popular with collectors, and this is reflected in a lower price. Later pens by Conklin such as the "Nozac" and "Symetrik" are very popular and collectible.

"Lucky curve" pen by Parker, 1916, **$32–231**

▲ Metal pens by Parker

This early hard-rubber ring-top pen by Parker is overlaid with gold-filled metal. It has a patented "lucky curve" feed to enhance ink flow – "lucky curve" was regularly promoted by Parker from 1905 to 1929 as a guarantee of top-quality design and performance. Such metal pens often suffer from brassing of the gold and corrosion of the section, so only examples in good condition are of significant value. The presence of a matching pencil (rare) and the leather case add to the value.

Waterman coding

- Waterman pens have numerical identity codes on the end of the barrels.
- The last number refers to the nib and pen size.
- The second to last digit describes the cap and filling details: 1=cone cap, 2=taper cap, 5=lever fill.
- The remaining numbers describe the overlay: 2= silver barrel only, 3=gold barrel only, 4=silver barrel and cap, 5=gold barrel and cap, 05=gold filled.

▼ Desk units

Pen holders for desktops were very popular in the 1920s. A range of designs was made, including ornate figures cast in bronze, attached to a marble or agate base and combined with clocks and lamps. This desk unit is by Parker and was one of a number of designs supplied with a "Duofold pen". In the 1930s Parker also made popular desk units in conjunction with the ceramics firm of Carlton.

"Sapphire" set by Conklin, 1929, **$132–198**

"Golden bear" desk unit by Parker, 1920s, **$165–330**

Streamlined pens

The financial turbulence of the late 1920s and early 1930s, sparked by the Wall Street Crash (1929), caused many pen companies to fold; most surviving firms were larger concerns, which succeeded by introducing new production techniques and styles. In line with the trend at this time for aerodynamically designed products, fountain pens with smooth lines in the "streamlined" style were a major innovation. Many such pens appear strikingly modern – the style proved so popular that it is still widely used today.

◀ Smooth lines

Sheaffer's elegant cigar-shaped pens in attractive plastic colors were vastly different from the old flat-topped pens. They were filled by means of a new plunger system, similar to systems used by Onoto and Eversharp Wahl, although lever fillers were also designed. They were produced in an attractive range of colors, in both striated and simulated pearl plastics, and with military or ordinary clips (as shown). Oversized pens are most prized, but the slimmer models are excellent writing instruments. The "Balance" model shown was reintroduced by Sheaffer in 1998.

Left to right: "Balance" pen by Sheaffer, 1930s, **$59–82**; "Abalone" pen by Sheaffer, 1930s, **$66–99**

▶ "Patrician" sets

Pens from the "Patrician" range, produced between 1929 and 1938 by Waterman, are extremely sought after by collectors. The rarest color is "black", but the most valued are "turquoise", "moss agate", and "emerald"; versions in "nacre" and "onyx" are less popular. Two designs of matching pencil were produced in the range. In general, sets are not very popular, as many collectors are only interested in purchasing the pen alone.

"Patrician" set by Waterman, c.1930s, **$1,072–1,650**

The recession
- Market activity in early 1929 held no terrors of economic recession for the "big four" of Eversharp Wahl, Parker, Sheaffer, and Waterman in the USA.
- New designs included the "Personal Point" by Eversharp Wahl, the first "Balance" pen by Sheaffer, the "Streamlined Duofold" by Parker, and the "Patrician" range by Waterman.

▼ **German manufacturers**

Pelikan and Montblanc were Germany's flagship makers, producing such high-quality, reasonably priced pens as the two shown below. The Pelikan "100" was the classic pen of the 1930s; it was made in a range of colors, with the green version shown being the most common and those with lizardskin or pearlescent bodies the most prized. The Montblanc pen is a button filler.

Transparent reservoir pen by Ford, 1932, **$330–495**

▲ **Branching out**

Ford were papermakers and specialists in blotting paper, and in 1932 used their name for an exquisite piston pen. Designed and patented by G. Stewart Vivian (a former employee of the Valentine firm), this pen was probably made by Wyvern and involves a transparent reservoir inside the barrel. The pen was made in at least four sizes, in "black", in "mottled", and with silver overlay.

Left to right: "100" by Pelikan, 1938, **$82–115**; pen by Montblanc, 1947, **$99–132**

▶ **Dorics**

The twelve-sided "Doric" pen by Eversharp Wahl was introduced in 1932. The jet example has a roller clip and an adjustable nib; the green marble version has a transparent barrel section. Both pens are lever fillers, but piston fillers were also made. The pen was produced in three lengths, and as extra-slim and oversized versions (highly prized). Some examples feature marbling or "spider's web" decoration.

Left to right: "Doric", 1932, **$165–247**; "Doric", 1938, **$115–132**

Pens of the 1930s

In the 1930s a number of innovations were introduced, notably in the USA, as major companies competed for the lion's share of the market. New filling systems, transparent barrels, and combination designs were all promoted as the effects of the depression receded. Canada became a main supplier of pens for the European market, Waterman made pens in a joint venture in France, but sadly many companies, such as both Carter and Chilton, faded from the scene in the USA as a result of very hard times.

▶ Combination designs

Although writing instruments combining pens and pencils had been produced before, designs with propelling pencils and fountain pens at opposite ends of the same barrel were novelties. These items were not particularly popular in the 1930s – perhaps because they had such poor ink capacities – and were regarded as pencils first and pens second. Many inferior-quality examples were made, although such firms as Sheaffer, Conklin (shown right), and Mabie Todd made quality products. Combination pens by Waterman and Parker exist but are very rare.

Combination
pen/pencil by
Conklin, 1930s,
$198–330

▶ New filling systems

In 1933 Parker promoted a new filling system with no sac, which it misleadingly claimed had no perishable parts. The system, known as "Vacumatic", involved a small pump, which expelled air from the barrel, so allowing ink to fill the pen; it was heavily advertised, and was successful partly because it coincided with the new range of pearlized plastics used for pen barrels. The increasingly varied range of sizes and patterns used also boosted sales. The "Golden Web" pen shown here, which was also made in a slimmer "Junior" version, was only produced for three years. This example is engraved, which generally reduces the value.

"Golden Web"
by Parker,
1935,
$198–280

Parker "Vacumatics"

- "Vacumatics" can be identified by the shape, cap design, and trim.
- Sizes include "Débutante", "Lady", "Major", "Maxima", and "Oversize".
- Patterns include "pearl", "marble", "Golden Web", and "Shadow-wave".
- Three pump systems were used: "Lockaway" (used 1933–8), "Speedline" (1939–41), and a disposable plastic pump (1942–9).
- By 1947 more than 6 million Parker "51 Vacumatics" had been produced.

▼ Elaborate finishes

Pens with imitation animal-skin caps and barrels were made in small numbers, often because the manufacturing cost of such plastics was very high. Mabie Todd and Waterman produced some very fine lizardskin patterns, while Conway Stewart and Parker both made distinctive herringbone-pattern pens. "Snakeskin" designs are also very sought after by collectors.

▼ Military clip pens

The American army demanded that any pens worn with uniform should be inconspicuous, so the major pen manufacturers responded with simple designs such as the pen featured below. These pens, where the clip is positioned at the very end of the cap came to be known as "top clip", "military clip", or sometimes "depression" pens due to their low prices. The 1932 "Moderne" and "Premier" by Parker are both good examples of simple, affordable "military clip" pens; both were made in novel colored plastics, often with a mosaic design.

"Top clip" pen by Parker, 1932, **$82–132**

"Lizardskin" pen by Waterman, 1937, **$165–247**

◄ "Lookalikes"

Most successful pens are imitated, often extremely convincingly. At first glance the two pens shown left appear to be Parker pens – a "Duofold" and a "Vacumatic" – but they are in fact copies by Plexor and Waterson. The most imitated pen is the "Senior Duofold", and such copies are now becoming collectible.

Left to right: Parker lookalike by Plexor, 1939, **$66–82**; Parker lookalike by Waterson, 1930, **$58–66**

Pens of the 1940s & 1950s

World War II had a great influence on fountain-pen production. Many designs that had been in the pipeline were brought out sooner than planned, and the development of new materials was accelerated. Some factories were re-directed to war-effort production, thereby encouraging sub-contracting and closer liaison between pen companies. However, apart from the striking examples of the "51" by Parker and "Skyline" by Eversharp Wahl, many designs on the market were the same in the 1940s as they had been in the 1930s.

◀ "Swan" pens

Mabie Todd was the leading penmaker between the two world wars, with its flagship brand "Swan". After World War II the firm continued to make quality pens with good flexible nibs, although many were of rather old-fashioned design. Some "Swan" pens used a unique leverless filling system, in which the pen was filled by twisting a knob; however, "Swan" lever fillers and eyedroppers (such as the rare export example shown) were also produced.

Left to right: "Swan" eyedropper by Mabie Todd, 1950s, **$25–49**; leverless "L210/60" by Mabie Todd, **$49–82**

▶ "Blackbird" pens

In addition to the pens discussed left, Mabie Todd produced less highly priced ranges, most of which had lever-filling systems and nickel trims. This model, from the popular "Blackbird" range, was made towards the end of Mabie Todd's fountain-pen-producing days. In 1951 Biro took a major shareholding in Mabie Todd, and the firm stopping making fountain pens in 1958.

"Blackbird" pen by Mabie Todd, 1953, **$49–66**

Nibs

- The main types of nib are fine, medium, broad, stub (italic), or oblique.
- Most nibs in British and American classic pens were 14-carat gold; continental European classic pens usually have 18-carat gold nibs.
- Iridium was first welded onto gold nibs for durability in 1834.
- Two-color nibs are usually made of platinum coated onto gold.
- In general, older nibs are more flexible than modern nibs.
- The nib normally accounts for one third of the material cost of a pen.

▼ British-made "Duofold" pens

The 1940s "Herringbone Duofold" shown below is basically the same design as the 1929 American-made "Duofold". This example is especially desirable because it is made from unusual patterned plastic and was produced in a small quantity only. The "Victory" range, made from 1935, is almost identical to the smaller "Duofolds" except for the trim. "Herringbone", "lizardskin", and "pearl" are the rarest "Duofolds", but "marbled lilac", "bronze", and "olive" British-made Parkers are excellent collector items.

"Herringbone Duofold" by Parker, 1940s, **$330–495**

▼ Pens by Valentine

The Valentine firm began to make pens in 1929 after acquiring the firms of Whytworth and Gold Nibs Ltd, but its most notable designs were produced after it was bought by Parker in 1947. Its lever- and button-fill pens were similar in materials and design to 1930s streamlined pens by Parker and Conway Stewart. Valentine pens were well made and frequently fitted with large, flexible nibs.

Lever-fill pen by Valentine, 1947, **$99–165**

◀ "Skyline" pens

The "Skyline" pen, introduced in 1941, was so called because it was advertised as ideal for air travel. It is a simple lever-fill pen and features a distinctive tapered barrel and clip in the style of a Greek helmet. Many variants were produced between 1941 and 1949, and in 1997 the same design was put back into production.

"Skyline" pen, 1945, **$82–132** (for a set)

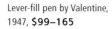

Modern pens

The fountain pen was still the most widely used writing instrument in schools until the early 1950s. The traditional gift on examination success or a birthday was a fountain pen, and this gift market was catered for by pen makers and stationers worldwide. Millions of Parker "51" pens, "Snorkels", Conway Stewarts, and Watermans were sold. The school and student pen market was especially significant, and Burnhams, Wyverns, and "Golden Platinum" pens were a regular feature on school desks.

▼ "51" pens

The Parker "51" is probably the most successful pen ever made. Robust and stylish with an excellent writing mechanism, it sold almost 42 million examples between 1939 and 1972. Earlier models used the "Vacumatic" filling system, and over 6 million examples were sold before the "Aerometric" system was introduced in 1947–8. The most collectible colors are "mustard", "nassau green", "plum", "forest green", and "tan". Also especially desirable are examples of the "Empire State" cap design.

"51" by Parker, 1953, **$115–165**

▼ Small pens

Although originally produced in the 1930s, Conway Stewart "Dinkies" were far more successful when reissued in the 1950s and marketed as gifts. The range included matching pencils, lead pencils, pocket knives, and even nail files, in attractive leather cases or wallets. Other companies such as Croxley and Unique also made miniature pens, and as their designs were less successful when first produced, they are now rare and desirable.

Left to right: mottled pen by Unique, 1934, **$66–82**; "Dinky" pens (x3) by Conway Stewart, 1947–53, **$49–58** (each)

The Parker "51"
- This pen was the winner of the US Fashion Academy Award in 1950.
- More than 30 different types of cap are known.
- Some of the very early models sold in the USA were button fillers (as opposed to "Vacumatic" or "Aerometric" fillers).
- An 18-carat gold "51" in top condition is worth over $1,650.
- Rolled-silver examples are rarer than gold ones.

▼ Pens by Wyvern
The Leicester-based firm of Wyvern was one of the oldest pen companies in Britain. After World War II the firm produced not only economical pens but also some unique models, including the leather-covered button filler shown. Wyvern pens were particularly popular with the British royal family – they were regularly presented to Palace staff, and George VI himself used a crocodile-skin model.

Button filler by Wyvern, 1950, **$148–198**

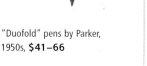

"Duofold" pens by Parker, 1950s, **$41–66**

▲ "Duofold" range
This range, first produced in the 1950s by Parker, was both affordable and highly practical. It was produced in solid colors – "green", "dark red", "blue", and "black" – and a variety of sizes, from the "Slimfold" to the "Duofold Maxima". "Duofold" pens are probably the most common ones to be found at car boot sales and antiques fairs, and they are among the best gold-nibbed classic pens available.

▶ Student pens
A typical student pen should be inexpensive, easily reparable, and robust enough to suffer the rigors of the classroom. Many such pens were sold by Mentmore, Unique, Burnham, Wyvern, Stephens, and Platinum. The two examples illustrated are a relatively rare pen by Stephens with a 14-carat gold nib, and a finely colored Burnham "No.44" with a gold nib (later ones had steel nibs).

Left to right: pen by Stephens, early 1950s, **$49–82**; "No.44" by Burnham, 1953, **$16–66**

Other modern pens

The invention of the reliable, inexpensive ballpoint pen totally changed the writing-equipment market. Companies who attempted to make fountain pens to compete in price with ballpoints in general did so only by a reduction in quality; in contrast, companies who focused on quality and promoted premium products on an international scale were vastly successful. From 1950, take-overs, mergers, the growth of new markets such as promotional pens, roller balls, and cartridges were all influential, although many excellent and collectible fountain pens were still produced.

◀ **"Pens For Men"**

In 1952 Sheaffer developed a unique filling system called the "snorkel", which was employed in the "Pen For Men" ("PFM") design in 1959. The "PFM" was produced in five different models over a period of fifteen years, and is currently one of the most collectible post-war pens by Sheaffer. It is an excellent writing pen and still widely used today, although it is becoming increasingly difficult to acquire parts for repairs, particularly nib units. The rarest colors are "gray", "blue", and "green".

"Pens For Men" by Sheaffer, 1962, **$124–239** (each)

▶ **"61" pens**

The Parker "51" was a hard act to follow, and when first introduced the "61" (perhaps owing to its innovative capillary filling system) was not a great success. Parker changed the design to a cartridge-and-converter system, but the pen, while an excellent writing instrument, still had defects – the plastic had a tendency to distort, and the shell arrow was easily dislodged. However, the "61", which was made in a fine range of colors, barrels, and caps, is highly collectible today. Notable examples include the "Cloud" range ("Stratus", "Cumulus", and "Cirrus"), "Consort", "Insignia", pens with unique "Rainbow" caps, and 9- and 18-carat gold models.

"61" pen/pencil set by Parker, 1974, **$82–132**

Ballpoint pens

- The first ballpoint pen was patented in the USA in 1888.
- The Hungarian Lazlo Biro produced the first reliable working ballpoint pen in 1940.
- By 1953 the ballpoint was no longer simply considered the poor relation of the fountain pen, and some fine examples were produced.
- Parker began making ballpoints in 1954.
- Papermate (part of Gillette) produces more than one billion ballpoints each year.

▼ The best of British design

The high-quality pens by Conway Stewart, particularly numbers "24", "27", "58", and "60", exemplify the best of British design. Although they were produced in large quantities, examples in unique colors, such as the "Cracked ice" pen shown (number "60"), or herringbone-pattern models are increasingly difficult to find in good condition. Matching pencils are often rarer than the pens.

"Cracked ice" pen by Conway Stewart, 1952, **$165–247**

▼ Ballpoint pens

Ballpoints made in the 1940s make interesting collectibles, but few are still in good working order. In contrast, many examples from the 1950s can still be used. Early Parker "T-ball jotters" are now collector items, as are most Parker "51", "61", and "75" ballpoints. As most fountain-pen makers had serious reservations about producing ballpoints, it is much more difficult to find them as part of 1950s sets than to find fountain pens or pencils.

Left to right: "Cisele 75" by Parker, 1969, **$99–115**; "Duofold Jotter" by Parker, 1950, **$25–50**

▶ Classic designs

The two piston pens shown right are both classic designs intended for the executive. The "146 Meisterstück" was introduced in 1948 and is still produced today. The "Magna" was a prized possession in its day, with a "No.7" two-color nib. It was also available as a lever filler and in candystripe colors, and was last produced in 1958.

Left to right: "146 Meisterstück" by Montblanc, 1970, **$115–214**; "Magna" by Onoto, 1955, **$247–412**

Unusual designs

Collectors are always looking for that rare or unique prototype, which can be a fascinating talking point when displaying a collection, and can quite often develop into a main area of collecting. Rare items are often those that were commercially unsuccessful when first produced, or special-purpose pens such as demonstrator models. Prototypes are often difficult to confirm as genuine, and it is probably more important to buy from a reputable source than to rely on "provenance".

▼ **Stylographic pens**
With narrow tubes as writing tips and wire inserts that control the flow of ink down the tube, stylographic pens have been produced since the mid-19thC. Reliable early examples were made in the 1870s by the firms of Caws, A.T. Cross, and McKinnon in the USA. In the early 20thC notable British makers included Onoto (see the hard-rubber examples left) and Conway Stewart (far left). In the 1930s the most popular American example was by Inkograph.

Left to right: "Ink Pencil" by Conway Stewart, 1925, **$41–66**; pen by Onoto, 1920, **$41–66**; pen by Onoto, 1918, **$33–41**

▶ **Glass-nibbed fountain pens**
The earliest glass nibs used in reservoir pens were made by Haro (Hans Roggenbuch). These early pens were very practical and robust and particularly well suited to producing carbon copies. During both world wars glass was widely used for nibs, as metals were in short supply. Many glass-nibbed pens were manufactured in Germany (see right) and Japan, although production was not exclusive to those countries – the British firm of Burnham produced a popular model in the 1930s and 1940s.

Pen by Palmtree, 1940s, **$25–33**

▼ Safety pens
Pens with retractable nibs are termed "safety" pens. The earliest designs, made by such firms as Moore and Conklin, featured nibs that simply slid back into the barrel, but later models, notably by Montblanc, Waterman, and Whytworth, used complex spiral systems. Elaborate Italian and French examples with overlay decoration are the most prized.

▼ Demonstrators
Salesmen used transparent pens to show customers not only the internal components of their wares but also how the filling systems worked. These intriguing items are now very collectible, especially examples of "Pens For Men" by Sheaffer, "Vacumatics" by Parker, and such elaborate examples as the rare Montblanc shown below.

Innovative designs
• Waterman and Moore both made "Trench" pens with ink pellets in the cap.
• Unusual novelty pens include "Mickey Mouse" by Inkograph and "Popeye" by the Eagle Pencil Co.
• Collectors should look out for innovative trap-door pens with covered nibs by Pullman.

▼ Elaborate mechanisms
This rare pen was made for Dunhill in the 1930s, possibly by Omas, and consists of two separate pens fitted into a conventional-size barrel. The two pens are linked by a mechanism, so that each nib extends alternately when the end of the barrel is twisted. Such unusual items command premium prices.

Two-in-one pen, 1930s, **$2,475–3,300**

Left to right: "Safety" pen by Waterman, 1920, **$132–165**; gold-overlay "Safety" pen by Waterman, 1925, **$330–495**

Left to right: demonstrator by Montblanc, 1960, **$825–1,155**; "51 Vacumatic" demonstrator by Parker, 1945, **$247–330**

Limited-edition pens

The production of a limited number of special-design pens with fancy packaging and documentation is a relatively new development in pen manufacture. Parker paved the way in the 1960s, and was followed in the 1990s by most major pen companies, including Sheaffer, Montblanc, Visconti, Aurora, Pelikan, and Omas. Most companies adopt themes such as sports, cities, historical events, or writers, or produce pens to commemorate calendar events – anniversaries or centennials; it is also popular to reissue short runs of classic pens from the past. In the early 1990s, limited-edition pens often sold out before production was completed, but as the number of pen makers introducing limited editions has grown, many collectors have become more discerning. However, limited editions are still regarded as one of the best investments in fountain-pen collecting.

◄ Sheaffer

Limited editions were not introduced by Sheaffer until 1995. The 18-carat gold commemorative pen shown far left was a faithful copy of the firm's successful 1920s flat-topped lever fill, and the "Lifetime Balance" (1997) was a copy of Sheaffer's 1929 "Balance" pen. Only 6,000 examples of each design were produced, plus an additional 100 transparent "Balances", which are even more exclusive than the example shown.

Left to right: commemorative pen, 1995, **$825–1,155**; "Lifetime Balance", 1997, **$660–1,155**

► Pelikan

All of Pelikan's limited editions are in the same style, as illustrated by the two examples shown right, although always in different materials and designs. Only 5,000 copies of "Blue Ocean" were made, of which 1,000 were sold as sets with a ballpoint pen, and a mere 888 copies of "Golden Dynasty" were produced. Other special editions by Pelikan include "Golf", "M900 Toledo", "Austria 1000", and "Concerto".

Left to right: "Blue Ocean", 1994, **$990–1,155**; "Golden Dynasty", 1994, **$1,650–1,980**

▼ "Author" pens by Montblanc

This "Agatha Christie" pen is one of a range of author-theme pens by Montblanc. Examples with silver trims are fairly common, and many are actually used to write with (unusual for a collector's edition); those with gold trims are rarer. Other pens in the series include "Hemingway" (1992), "Oscar Wilde" (1994), "Voltaire" (1995), "Alexandre Dumas" (1996), and "Dostoyevsky" (1997). The packaging and documentation are lavish and play an important part in the appeal.

"Agatha Christie" pen, 1993, **$742–825**

Collectible designs

• Parker introduced its first limited edition, the "Spanish Treasure 75", in 1965.
• Waterman's first limited edition (1989) honored the bicentenary of the 1789 French Revolution.
• Montblanc introduced its first limited edition in 1992; its special runs are restricted to 4,810 copies.
• The most exclusive limited editions include Parker's gold "Snake" pen (250 made), Visconti's "Taj Mahal" in ivory and gold (88 made), Aurora's gold "Benvenuto Cellini" (199 made), and Montegrappe's "Gold Dragon" (100 made).

▶ "People & history" pens by Montblanc

This series, promoted by Montblanc as a vehicle for celebrating beauty, inspiring creativity, and advancing culture, is one of its most imaginative and celebrated ranges. In addition to "Semiramis" (inspired by the Assyrian Queen) and the blue filigree "Prince Regent" shown right, the range included such designs as "Lorenzo de Medici" and "Louis XIV".

Left to right: "Semiramis", 1996, **$1,485–1,980**; "Prince Regent", 1995, **$2,970–4,125**

▶ Parker

The first limited editions by Parker were based on existing models such as the "75" or "105", but they were made in materials with romantic connections – silver recovered from shipwrecks, and brass from notable liners. The "Charles and Diana" was made to commemorate the royal wedding (1981).

Left to right: "Queen Elizabeth", 1977, **$825–1,155**; "Charles and Diana", 1981, **$660–990**

Pencils: basics

Charcoal was used in cave paintings, metallic lead styluses were used two thousand years ago to mark paper and papyrus, and graphite-based drawing-sticks have been known since Elizabethan times. Graphite is soft and needs a support tube for protection or a cover to prevent the hands from becoming soiled. The invention of hard "lead" paved the way for wood-encased pencils and retractable propelling pencils. Until recently, pencils have not been highly valued, but a wider appreciation of the craftsmanship involved in producing pencils, and of the intricate workings of mechanical examples, has elevated values and sparked collector interest.

▼ **Mechanical pencils**

The two diagrams below illustrate the components of typical mechanical pencils from the 19thC (left) and the 20thC (right). On most 19thC examples the outer case is a thin silver or gold tube. In the 20thC it became more standard for the case to be based on a plastic barrel with a simple inexpensive mechanism fitted.

▼ **Porte crayons and cedar holders**

The porte crayon was a metal tube designed to hold a "lead" (a thick graphite rod), often with a sliding mechanism to extend the former. Cedar holders, with brass-threaded inserts, were made to hold whole wooden pencils (often known as "cedars"). Most are between 5cm and 7.5cm (2–3in) in length. Value is determined by design, size, and maker.

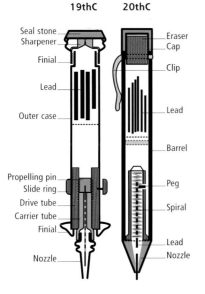

19thC | 20thC

Seal stone
Sharpener
Finial
Lead
Outer case
Propelling pin
Slide ring
Drive tube
Carrier tube
Finial
Nozzle

Eraser
Cap
Clip
Lead
Barrel
Peg
Spiral
Lead
Nozzle

Left to right: cedar holder by Mordan, 1840, **$33–49**; porte crayon, 1817, **$247–330**; heavy cedar holder, 1885, **$49–66**

▼ Screw and slide mechanisms

Screw mechanisms were used by watch and instrument makers in the 17thC, and were probably also applied to writing items at that time. However, the first recorded use of such a screw mechanism in pencils was detailed in the Hawkins and Mordan patent of 1822. The earliest example known is marked 1823, and such early pencils are rare and valuable. Early pencils can be dated fairly accurately by their decoration, the design of their finials, and their stub-shaped nozzles. Later pencils have more ornate engraving, which is a major factor in determining the value.

Left to right: early pen/pencil by Mordan, 1823, **$825–990**; pencil by Mordan Riddle, 1825, **$330–412**

▼ Open-ended combinations

Designs combining a pen and pencil at opposing ends of tubes were diverse. Examples range from inexpensive tinplate or nickel "penny pushers" (sold originally for only a penny), which combined dip pens and wooden pencils, to luxury versions combining pens and mechanical pencils in silver and gold.

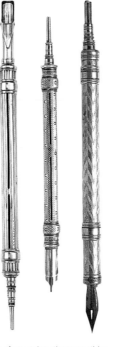

Left to right: silver pencil by Mordan, 1825, **$412–495**; pencil by Cunningham & Smart, 1850, **$115–132**; tinplate pen/pencil, 1880, **$8–25**

Leads
- As the graphite sticks used in early propelling pencils wore away very quickly, makers began to experiment to produce a harder "lead". A process of mixing graphite, silicate, and a binder, then extruding the mix into fine rods and firing them in a kiln, was developed c.1790 by both the firm of Conté in France and that of Hardmuth in Germany.
- Different ratios of filler and binder determine the hardness of the "leads".

▼ One-ended combinations

Combination designs with the pen and pencil at the same end were popular even into the 20thC. These examples were made by Mordan and could be used with metal nibs and quill slips; similar combinations, especially those by Fairchild, were very popular in the USA. On some models, pulling or twisting the barrel exposed delicate slider pins to push out the pen or pencil; other designs featured intricate twisting mechanisms, which exposed the pen when turned clockwise and the pencil when twisted anti-clockwise.

Combination pens by Mordan, 1880, **$247–412** (each)

Mechanical pencils

Mechanical pencils were manufactured both by small concerns such as silversmiths, who bought in mechanisms and made and fitted "pencil cases", and by large manufacturers such as Mordan, Butler, Fairchild, and Hicks, whose main business was the production of mechanical pencils. The design of pencils is therefore diverse, particularly as leads and nozzle sizes were not standardized.

▶ Miniature pencils

Small decorative pencils, such as the examples shown right, were manufactured mainly in Britain and USA, and are fairly readily available today. They include slim sliders, telescopic designs, and examples decorated with semi-precious jewels and enameling. The mechanisms in pencils are generally very delicate and often do not work, in which case they will be of very little value other than as spare parts.

Left to right (top to bottom): small slider, 1890, **$41–58**; 9-carat pencil by Mordan, 1900, **$66–99**; celluloid pencil by Hicks, 1890, **$99–132**; pencil by Fairchild, 1890, **$132–165**; enameled telescopic pencil, 1900, **$124–157**; small carpenter pencil, 1900, **$25–33**

▼ Niche collecting areas

Some enthusiasts concentrate on collecting novelty pencils, of which there is a vast range. Designs include examples in the shape of owls, dogs, birds, pistols, rifles, spinning tops, golf clubs, screws, and nails. One popular area of collecting is Egyptian-design pencils, including obelisk- and sphinx-themed ones as well as the mummy-shaped design shown right. Most are enameled, like the example illustrated, but watch out for crudely cast models. Combination items of pencils with knives, rulers, and tooth-picks are another niche collecting area. The combined knife and pencil shown far right was produced in the USA by Edward Todd in conjunction with J. Wolstenholme of Sheffield.

Left to right: "Mummy" pencil, 1890, **$132–181**; knife and pencil by Todd, 1900, **$115–148**

Tricolor pencils, 1890,
$148–247 (each)

▲ Tricolor pencils

Models with three separate pencils (red, blue, and black) in one case are known as "tricolor" pencils. Most are made of silver – gold ones are rare. Some collectors specialize in the variety of mechanism used to extend the tricolor pencils. The two silver pencils shown are sliders; other examples have button-release mechanisms, telescopic extensions, three-sided sliders, or three-segment twists. Good condition is important, so look carefully at the enamel, and check that the mechanism is in working order. Double and quadruple pencils were also made.

▼ Desk and writing-case sets

Many mechanical pencils were produced as part of desk or writing-case sets with matching pens, seals, and knives. Examples found separately, such as the tortoiseshell-and-gold pencil and the bulbous American model shown below, are still very collectible.

Left to right: pencil by Vickery, 1880, **$115–148**; silver pencil with chain link, 1910, **$66–115**

FACT FILE

Makers' marks
• The majority of British pencils were made in London or Birmingham; most feature the mark of the maker or retailer.
• Major names include: Willmore, Vale, Riddle, Baker, Moseley, Yard-O-Led, Asprey, Sucklings, Manton, Villiers & Jackson, Lund, and Walker & Hall.

▼ Major makers

Although the number of major makers producing mechanical pencils was small, the number of designs created was vast. Mordan's 1895 catalog features 195 different pencils; Baker's 1905 catalog includes 210 designs. The most popular examples were the plainer ones, as shown below. The "Torpedo" design is a twist-action pencil made in gold and silver; the design in the centre is in engine-turned silver, but was also sold as a silver-plated pencil, and the "Popular" pencil has an unusual screw mechanism.

Left to right: "Torpedo" pencil, 1920s, **$82–132**; engine-turned pencil, 1930, **$41–82**; "Popular" pencil, 1890, **$82–165**

Rare pencils

A vast array of pencils was produced in Europe and the USA, including some highly decorative, de-luxe designs (usually special commissions) that were more akin to beautiful pieces of jewelry than functional writing items. Particularly exclusive designs, including some novelty creations, were produced by leading jewelers in New York's Fifth Avenue, London's Regent Street, and Paris's Avenue Foch. Most were never featured in catalogs but were unique, one-off creations, made for special customers; this type of pencil is rare and correspondingly valuable today.

▼ **Famous names**
Neither Roland Cartier nor Tiffany & Co. produced pencils as part of its standard range, so the examples by these firms shown below (a 14-carat gold pencil by Cartier, and a silver Art Deco pencil by Tiffany) were made as special commissions. The third pencil, with a twist extension in a silver repoussé case, was made by Hicks, and as a less exclusive design is not as valuable as the other two pens, although still very desirable.

Left to right: pencil by Hicks **$165–198**; telescopic pencil by Tiffany, 1920s, **$412–577**; pencil by Cartier, 1950, **$330–495**

▶ **De-luxe combination designs**
The "Traveler" shown right is a combination of a pen and a pencil with the addition of a mini thermometer on the barrel and a compass on the top finial. The ivory casing features some small cracks, but these will scarcely affect the value as the pencil is so rare. One variant of this design is known with a metal case.

"Traveler" by Mordan, 1890, **$495–660**

▼ "Dropper" pencils
The "dropper" was first introduced in 1911. The pressing of a button on the top of the case causes the pencil to drop down, ready for use. Many examples made by Mordan had seven-sided outer cases, which could adapt into perpetual calendars. This unusual 15-carat gold round pencil was probably made by Mordan for Vickery's Regent Street store. Perpetual calendars add value to most pencils.

▼ Telescopic designs
This simply designed pencil was made by Hicks of New York. It contains a silver ruler and measuring dividers, and was probably either sold at an exclusive New York shop or specifically commissioned, as such large silver pencils were not typical of Hicks's designs. The value is due largely to the novelty combination.

▶ Telescopic designs
Rarity is something that most collectors seek ardently, and this telescopic pencil with an outer case decorated with a selection of international flags is particularly unusual and desirable – hence its high value. The enamel shows some damage, which affects the value although not dramatically.

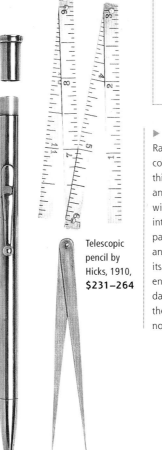

"Dropper" pencil with perpetual calendar, hallmarked "Vickery", 1915, **$247–412**

Telescopic pencil by Hicks, 1910, **$231–264**

Telescopic pencil by Mordan, 1890, **$412–660**

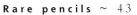

Modern pencils

Modern propelling pencils, manufactured to match pens in sets, as well as for use as promotional items, have become increasingly popular since the introduction of inexpensive plastics and mechanisms in the 1940s. Separate pencils were often promoted as corporate gifts before the advent of the ballpoint pen, and silver or gold quality pencils were often given as traditional retirement or leaving presents.

▼ **Yard-O-Led**

Early pencils by Yard-O-Led are very collectible, useable, and offer excellent value for money. Round-, square-, and (rare) triangular-barreled models are illustrated below, but the firm produced a very wide range of designs. Other versions include a rare "heavy" pencil, and a small half-length design known as the "Yard-O-Lette". The hexagonal "Diplomat", a popular post-war model, is almost exactly the same today as when first produced in 1947.

Left to right: "Yard-O-Lette", 1950, **$33–49**; round-barreled "Aristocrat", 1955, **$33–41**; triangular-barreled pencil, 1950, **$99–132**

▼ **Eversharp Wahl**

In 1917 Wahl, a shrewd machine manufacturer, purchased the Japanese patent for the mechanical pencil and continued to produce the same design for the next 40 years. These pencils were very simple propel-only designs, and their value will depend on the rarity, decoration, and material of the outer cases. Variations, including the lady's gold-filled ringtop, the large, red-and-black hard-rubber version, and the standard, clipped, gold-filled pencil, are illustrated right. Some of the most desirable models, such as the "Greek Key" design were made with matching pens.

Left to right: lady's ringtop, 1940, **$16–33**; hard-rubber pencil, 1925, **$49–66**; gold-filled pencil, 1935, **$33–49**

▼ Different types of lead

One of the most complex aspects of collecting pencils is the bewildering variety of lead diameters and nozzle systems used. The diameter of pencils by Mordan is usually indicated by codes on the nozzles, but although these can be matched with original leads they do not correspond to modern leads. Modern leads are usually 0.3mm, 0.5mm, 0.7mm, and 0.9mm, but most older pencils used 0.8mm, 1mm, and 1.5mm leads, so pencil collectors avidly search for and collect old leads. Leads by Hardmuth and Faber are quite common, and pencils by Yard-O-Led take 1.18mm leads, which are still available.

Left to right: box of leads by Faber, 1900, **$10–16**; box of leads by Mordan, 1890, **$10–16**

▶ Plastic pencils

Most major fountain-pen manufacturers also produced matching pencils for sale in sets. Surprisingly, the pencil usually adds little to the value of the set, except in the case of very rare examples; prices of separate pencils can hence be very affordable. Most examples feature simple peg-and-spiral mechanisms, which allow for both propelling and repelling actions.

Left to right: "Balance" by Sheaffer, 1930, **$25–49**; "jade" flat top by Sheaffer, 1928, **$25–49**; "ripple" by Waterman, 1930, **$16–33**

Sampson Mordan

- In his very first patent, dated 1822, Mordan was described as a "portable pen maker".
- The partnership (1823–37) between Mordan and the stationer Riddle laid down the foundations for the mechanical-pencil market.
- From *c.*1860 until 1930 mechanical pencils were known in popular parlance as "mordans".
- The differences in makers' marks helps the dating of pencils without hallmarks.

▼ Advertising pencils

Although pens were made for promotions, pencils were more popular in the 1930s and 1940s as free gifts. The variety of such pencils is vast, since they were used to promote items as varied as food products, businesses, and special events.

Advertising pencils, 1930s and 1940s, **$5–25** (each)

45

Traveling inkwells & penners

Writing equipment designed for itinerant scribes – artisans who traveled with their writing equipment to record legal or civil events – dates back many centuries. Until the 17thC most inkwells were portable – it only became popular to produce inkwells for use in one place from the 18thC. Pens (quills or reeds) were carried in penners, ink was kept in a separate inkpot or horn, and in the 18thC any suitable box such as a tobacco box was used to store quills. With the increase in touring in the 19thC and into the 20thC many writing items in increasingly sophisticated designs were manufactured specifically for travel.

▼ Penners

Penners were popular from 1700. They consisted of a compartment for a short quill, a pounce holder, and an inkwell, which was normally stuffed with wool to absorb the ink and reduce leakage. Two horn examples are shown below, and the disassembled penner is marked "1795". Similar items were made in leather, brass, bone, silver (rare), and even porcelain (very rare).

Front to back: disassembled penner, 1795, **$412–742**; assembled penner, 1800, **$330–660**

▼ Traveling inkwells

This double inkwell with a telescopic brass pen is typical of inkwells made in the 1860s. Most examples are covered in morocco leather, and the wells feature hinged lids with sprung leather seals. Rectangular double travelers were also produced. Single travelers of the same construction are very common; most feature simple buttons to open covering lids and clasps to release well lids.

Double traveling inkwell, 1860s, **$132–247**

Exotic inkwells

Qalandans such as the example shown below have been used in the Middle East since the 15thC. Arabic script lends itself to wonderful calligraphy, and Middle Eastern scribes are prolific writers, mainly using reed pens. Ornate qalandans engraved with quotations from the *Koran* in silver and gold inlay are most prized, but the majority are simple brass pen holders both with and without attached ink containers. The ink was often in powdered form in a muslin bag. Genuine qalandans are very rare – the majority of examples seen at antiques fairs were made for tourists passing through the Suez Canal or visiting the Pyramids.

Qalandan, 1850,
$115–148

Ransome's patent inkwells

In this design, with a button lid-release, the ink is contained in a glass bottle, which is held shut with a leather seal. Both metal-framed models and larger wells cast in wooden frames were made. The main advantage of the design was that it could be folded for packing or erected to stand on a desk as a dipping well.

Ransome's patent inkwell, 1860,
$115–198

Ink

• Until the 1860s ink was a corrosive liquid manufactured from a combination of oak gall, iron salts, gum arabic, and vinegar; after this time less harmful aniline dyes were increasingly used.

• Materials used to contain ink must be acid resistant, so the majority of inkwells are made from lead, horn, enamel, or glass. Inkwells produced from more susceptible materials, such as brass or wood, usually feature protective interior linings.

Traveling ink bottles

In the mid-19thC ink was usually carried in a small bottle in a lignum vitae case. By the mid-20thC the range of materials available to makers was far greater, and glass ink bottles can be found enclosed in bakelite, wood, or metal cases. Bottles by Parker, Mabie Todd, Waterman, and Onoto are highly prized, particularly if the labels and bottle lids are in good condition.

Bakelite bottle for Stephens writing ink, 1935, **$33–41**

Glass & porcelain inkwells

The range of glass and porcelain inkwells and inkstands is vast. Values may reflect the status of the manufacturer rather than the design of the inkwell, but with all examples good condition is vital. Most examples were produced in the 19thC, but reproductions abound, so careful examination of every design is vital.

▼ Glass inkwells

Glass, probably the material best suited to holding ink, was popularly used for ink bottles, many of which doubled as inkwells. The affordable, practical well shown below left was used until the 1930s, and the round example with a cone-shaped center was a catalog item from the 1830s. Many wells had glass inserts, although most school wells were made of pottery, as this was less costly. Some unusual non-spilling inkwells in heavy glass were made in the USA by the firm of Sangbusch.

▼ Square inkwells

The square inkwell is probably the most prevalent inkwell design for desk units and writing boxes. Not all square inkwells are of simple design – some are particularly ornate, in matched pairs, or in colored glass in shades of emerald-green, light green, or blue. Most examples measure 3.75cm (1½in) square – larger sizes (up to 10cm/4in) fetch a premium. Chipped or cracked designs are worth little, so check very carefully for damage.

Square inkwell, 1900, **$33–66**

Left to right: inkwell, 1850s, **$5–8**; round inkwell, 1830, **$16–25**

Bird's nest inkwell, 1890, **$82–132**

▲ Staffordshire wares

Many pottery and porcelain firms in Staffordshire produced inkwells as part of their ranges. The bird's nest shown above is typical of designs featuring animals and birds – similar models include inkwells in the shape of swans, dogs, and, rarer, parrots, and herons. Many examples have kiln cracks or have been repaired (sometimes badly), and most designs are unmarked, so buy carefully.

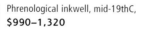

Phrenological inkwell, mid-19thC, **$990–1,320**

▲ Phrenological inkwells

This inkwell with a central well and two quill holders is a classic design, depicting the phrenological areas of the brain. It was made in Staffordshire in the mid-19thC. Gold-and-blue-lined examples are known as are smaller inkwells without the base. Such unique wells are very rare and valuable.

▼ Filling systems

This rare marked fish-shaped example by Perry & Co. is based on a syphon system. Ink is poured into the well when the latter is turned upside down; when the well is re-inverted a constant level of ink is exposed. Many similar designs were made, and 1930s American desk units use a similar principle with an ink bottle as the reservoir.

Inkwell by Perry, 1874, **$297–330**

Metal & novelty inkwells

The earliest metal inkstands, many of which are intricately formed and assembled, date from the 17thC. Silver, pewter, and tin were most typical, although examples were also made from cast brass, bronze, and spelter (a combination of zinc, tin, and lead). The majority of metal wells, except the earliest 17thC pewter and silver designs, employed a protective, non-corrodable insert to hold the ink.

▼ Rare pewter inkwells
This rare Irish pewter inkwell, which was probably made in Dublin by Sylvester Savage, has a pounce drawer, a wafer drawer, and four holes for quills. The ink was contained in a pot or glass bottle in the top section. Wells such as this are occasionally found with double ink compartments. Similar inkstands were made in The Netherlands with a well, a wafer drawer, and usually a more curved, Rococo design.

Inkwell, 1780,
$412–577

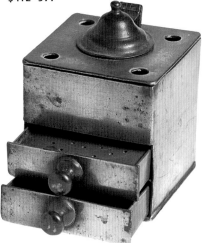

▲ Typical pewter inkwells
The example featured above is highly typical of the type of pewter inkwell used in banks and offices from the late 18thC to the 20thC. Holes for quills (later used for steel dip pens) surround a central glass well. Sometimes such inkwells are attached to a large pewter plate and referred to as "ship's" or "captain's" wells. The example above bears the coat-of-arms of George IV (reigned 1820–30), which probably signifies that it was used in a government office.

Inkwell,
c.1830,
$41–82

▶ Figural inkwells

The piece featured right depicts Daniel Lambert, the heaviest man in England in 1800, who was famed at the court of George III (reigned 1760–1820) for his huge appetite. It is an early example of a painted cast-iron well and is quite rare. Less ornamental cast-iron wells, often incorporating pen stands, were used in offices.

Figural inkwell, c.1820, **$165–412**

▶ Animal wells

Inkwells modeled as animals and birds are very popular among collectors. Many, such as the boar's head shown right, are made of spelter. Birds (particularly owls), dogs, and camels are all fairly common. French and Austrian wells command premium prices, and examples in bronze are usually more detailed and accurately cast than those in gun metal. Collectors should watch out for damaged wells, as repair is tricky and if carried out unprofessionally can detract from the value.

Boar's head inkwell, 1890, **$132–148**

Metal wells & stands

• The oldest known English silver inkstand is a 1630 well, pounce, and quill holder made by WR of London.
• The Huguenot silversmith Paul de Lamerie made exquisite inkstands in the 1730s, which are extremely desirable but rare – one sold in 1998 in New York achieved $1,248,555.
• Britannia metal (an alloy similar to pewter) was used for wells and stands, notably lidded wells used at the Treasury.

▼ Capstan inkwells

The capstan shape was popular for silver inkwells from c.1880 to 1920, with examples varying from 2.5cm (1in) to 17.5cm (7in) in diameter. Some had grooves for pens, ornate lids (for example, in tortoiseshell or with engraved decoration), or were made as part of boxed sets. The silver is often thin and easily damaged, and hinges are difficult to repair, so examples in good condition command a premium.

Capstan inkwell with pen, 1907, **$198–231**

Special-design inkwells

A number of highly decorative and now very collectable inkwells were designed to special commission; some were made as "show-stoppers" to be displayed at exhibitions. The examples illustrated all combine porcelain or glass with metal, making them more robust and practical; however, most of these highly decorative inkwells were produced for decoration only and would rarely have been used.

Inkwell
by Willmore,
1840,
**$1,155–
1,485**

▲ Opaque-glass inkwells
This inkwell was produced by the Birmingham maker Joseph Willmore. The well itself is made of opaque blue glass. The silver frame is hand formed, the leaves have been engraved individually before being joined to the stem, and the lid is decorated with a repoussé design. Such an item would have taken about a week to produce and would have been a premium piece in 1840 – hence the high value. Silversmiths often produced such ornate pieces as this for medals and competitions.

▼ Staffordshire designs
This bell-shaped, metal-mounted inkwell with a glazed floral design and inner porcelain liner was produced by the firm of Taylor, Tunnicliffe & Co. in Hanley, Staffordshire. This piece measures 9cm (3½in) in height, and such large inkwells are particularly prized among collectors. This example features a design mark and can consequently be accurately dated.

Porcelain
inkwell by
Taylor,
Tunnicliffe &
Co., 1883,
$330–412

Large inkstand,
1839, **$577–742**

British registered design marks

- Diamond-shaped marks were used from 1842 to 1883 and help collectors to date items.
- From 1842 to 1867 the year is given at the top of the diamond; from 1868 to 1883 the year is featured on the right of the mark.
- Letters signifying the year of production are not in alphabetical order, so check details in a reference table.

▼ Hydraulic inkwells

Hydraulic inkwells were fairly common in Britain and France from the 1840s. The level of the ink in the front spout could be adjusted by raising and lowering a block of porcelain inside the well. The novel example shown below, which has a cast-bronze base, features a bell on the top to ring for attention.

▲ Large inkstands

The impressive gilded French inkstand shown above, with a pounce pot, wafer container, rack for five pens or quills, a hydraulic well, and a tray for trinkets, would have taken pride of place on a large desk. Large inkstands are quite rare, but still not very popular with collectors as they are bulky. This example is stamped "Encrier Pompe Medaille D'Argent 1839", indicating that the design won a silver medal at the ninth Paris Exhibition in 1839.

Hydraulic inkwell,
1860, **$330–495**

Inkstand by Sèvres, 1764,
$2,062–2,475

▲ Sèvres

The royal porcelain factories at Sèvres produced some stunning pieces, including this urn-shaped inkstand hand-painted with four landscape scenes and mounted in metal. The condition is excellent, which combined with such a famous factory explains the high value. Quality pieces are very rare, and fakes and copies abound, so it is vital to have such pieces identified by an expert to check authenticity.

Desk accessories

In the early 19thC it was typical to embark upon a lengthy procedure of assembling accessories – preparing the parchment or paper, and arranging the desk and writing instruments – before starting to write. By the end of the 19thC such laborious processes as sprinkling pounce onto the paper to prepare it for absorbing ink, and marking out paper, had become obsolete, and the accessories used to carry them out had been dispensed with. As a result such items may now be rarer than the writing instruments themselves.

Left to right:
pounce
pot, 1800,
$115–330;
pounce pot,
1850,
$82–165

▲ Pounce pots
Pots for holding pounce are distinctive because they normally have perforated concave surfaces so that the expensive pounce could be rubbed back into the pot and reused. Also called "sanders" (after gum sandarach, which was a component of pounce), they were standard items on most inkstands. Individual pots were normally made of wood, porcelain, and pewter, and are often mistaken for sugar-shakers, nutmeg pots, or pepper-pots. The two examples shown are a Swedish burr-wood pot (left), and a more recent coquilla-nut design (right).

▼ Blotters
Ink was slow to dry on oily vellum, but was quickly absorbed into poor-quality, unsized (uncoated) paper. Consequently, such rough paper was probably used for blotting in the 18thC alongside powder or pounce, although it was only sold specifically as "blotting paper" from c.1840. Old pads, rocker blotters, and advertising blotters are very popular with collectors. Chalk was also used to help blotting, as illustrated by the unusual American roller blotter below.

Roller blotter,
1880,
$49–99

Pounce

- Pounce is a mix of gum sandarach and ground pumice or cuttlefish.
- Pounce was essential for treating writing surfaces, as parchment was often very greasy and paper poorly sized, which made it difficult to write on.
- When pounce was rubbed onto a surface, it either absorbed grease or, in the case of paper, created a "size" to give a less absorbent surface on which to write.

▼ Rulers

Although most 19thC rulers were simple, round ebony rods (see below left), some, for example rulers in silver or brass, were more elaborate. The postal ruler below right was overlaid with a transfer giving details of postal rates and some examples feature scenes or tartan designs, or are combined with pencils, erasers, or perpetual calendars. Attractive hexagonal rulers in crystal and flat ivory rulers are particularly desirable.

Left to right: ruler, 1900, . **$7–13**; postal ruler, 1890, **$66–132**

Paper-clip by Aumont, 1896, **$495–660**

▲ Paper-clips

The most common clips were made of cast or pressed brass in the form of gloved hands, scarab beetles, or fingers. Carved wooden clips are relatively rare and often have storage areas for stamps. The exquisite example in tortoiseshell and silver shown above was made by Henri Aumont. Collectors should take care, as most examples – even those with deceptively rusty springs – are reproductions. Good-quality paper-clips normally feature the stamp of the manufacturer.

▼ Pen wipes & brushes

Dip pens were cleaned before and after use on specially made wipes or brushes, to remove any residue. Circular wipes measuring approximately 5cm (2in) in diameter often feature a figural stud in the center. Many brushes are part of traveling inkwells or in silver or porcelain mounts in the forms of animals. The brush shown below also serves as a pen stand.

Brush with pen stand by Gourdel, Vales & Co., 1904, **$148–198**

Postal equipment & seals

Until recently, completing letters or formal documents and dispatching them was a lengthy process, involving all types of postal equipment. Before it became common practice to send letters in envelopes, they were sealed using wax and usually branded with the crest of the sender, using a variety of personalized devices. Circular, thin stickers (known as "wafers") were also used to seal letters; these were also typically marked with crests. The range of postal equipment available to collectors is vast, and includes stamp holders, tapers and other devices used to melt wax, seals, sealing-stick holders, and "wafers".

▼ Stamp holders

The most common stamp holders are envelope-shaped silver pockets and small boxes with sloping sections. Stamp boxes were made in a range of materials, including brass, silver, porcelain, wood, and ivory. The two shown are unusual designs. The silver pencil with the stamp roll is an American design; the hallmarked silver pouch holds two different-sized stamps.

Left to right: pencil and stamp holder, 1900, **$165–198**; pouch, 1905, **$66–82**

▼ Wax-melting devices

Sealing wax was often melted using tapers or small candles, and miniature candle holders were often produced as part of inkstands. Taper holders, known as "wax-jacks", usually had flexible wick-like heavy string wound around metal bobbins. The top of the brass spring-loaded taper holder made by Thomas Wharton shown here acts as a snuffer, and the base features a hatched seal.

Taper holder by Wharton, 1846, **$165–198**

Left to right: hatched seal, 1790, **$577–660**; hatched seal, 1860, **$26–33**

FACT FILE

Sealing wax
• Wax for pre–19thC seals was a mix of beeswax and resin, colored red with vermilion or green with verdigris. Later sealing wax is not wax at all but a mixture of shellac and vermilion.
• "Wafer" seals were made from flour, egg white, or gelatinous isinglass, and normally dyed with a vermilion colorant; most were 2cm (¾in) in diameter.

▼ Sealing sticks
Sticks of wax used to seal documents were often brittle, so many were kept in protective tubes with slider mechanisms to push out the wax. The earliest 18thC holders are often confused with pencil holders, as they had round cross sections; most later holders were square. The example featured left is an unusual hallmarked silver model with an attached extendable taper.

Sealing-stick holder, 1895, **$198–231**

▲ "Wafer" seals
Prior to the "penny" post, the cost of a letter was based on weight, so it was usual to fold the letter on itself and seal it with a thin, sticky "wafer". The wafer was positioned on the letter and moistened, and a hatched seal was then pressed onto the fold and held until the wafer adhered. Hatched seals were produced either as separate items, as in the case of the ebony-handled one above, or as part of a compendium (for example, the French ebony-and-ivory example also shown above).

▼ Seals
Seals were used to authenticate documents. The term "seal" can refer to the wax impression that secures the document or to the instrument used to make the impression; the latter is often known as the "seal matrix" to differentiate between the two. Seal matrices are specialist collecting items in their own right, with a wide variety of designs cut out in silver (see below), brass, steel, and hardstone, and attached to wooden, ivory, or metal handles. Different types of seal include fob seals and ring seals (signet rings), as well as finial seals on pencils, pens, and sealing-wax holders; most are engraved with initials, a crest, or a shield.

Seal by Mordan, 1865, **$132–148**

Advertising & display

George S. Parker (of Parker fame) informed his agents in 1904 that "a pen well presented is half sold", highlighting the importance of display and packaging. The well-lit, elaborate cabinets that are familiar in pen shops today show off products to their best advantage, but lack the charm of the mirrored, mahogany cabinets of yesteryear. Old display cabinets are much sought after by collectors but, like sheet-steel signs and quality merchandising items and catalogs, they are rare and at a premium.

▼ **Counter-display cabinets**
The display cabinet for nibs shown here features details of the different Gillott steel nibs for sale on small celluloid plaques in each compartment. Old wooden display cases for "Swan", Waterman, or Parker pens, especially small cases, are most popular with collectors.

Display cabinet by Gillott, 1890, **$165–247**

▶ **Novelty display units**
The value of wall-display units such as the Stephens thermometer shown depends on the condition and the company. Display material connected with Waterman, Parker, "Swan", and Onoto sparks much greater interest than material linked with lesser-known makers.

Advertising thermometer, 1938, **$330–412**

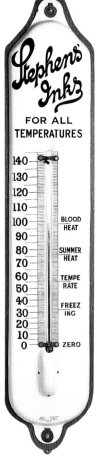

▼ Promotional items

Many makers produced ranges of eye-catching wares to help promote their pen products. Parker commissioned a range of porcelain wares in the style of its "Quink" ink bottles, including desk tidies, letter racks, and biscuit jars. Ceramic pens were produced by Parker and Pelikan, and the latter used porcelain pelican birds to advertise its products.

Magazine advertisement for pens by Parker, 1920s, **$5–16**

▲ Display signs

Large wooden display signs or billboards intended to attract customers into shops are very rare, because most have weatherbeaten or have been eaten by woodworm. Smaller wooden signs intended for display inside shops are more common. Models of giant pens (Waterman) and giant nibs (Sheaffer) are popular among collectors and dealers alike but rarely come up for sale.

"Quink" bottles by Parker, 1960, **$33–66**

▲ Brochures & catalogues

Original advertisements such as the one above, which featured in *National Geographic*, as well as old trade magazines or brochures are of interest to most collectors. Old manuals, catalogs, house magazines, price lists, or promotional material, particularly items connected with such major firms as Parker, Waterman, Mordan, and Gillott command premium prices.

Glossary

barrel main body of a pen where the ink or ink reservoir is stored

"Big Red" name for hard-rubber or "Permanite" orange-colored "Duofold Senior" pen made by Parker from 1924 to 1929

blind cap decorative screw-on cover at the end of the pen barrel to cover the filling button

blow filler pen with a filling system in which air is blown through a hole to depress the rubber sac

brassing wearing away of gold plating to reveal the base metal (copper or brass) beneath

button small brass unit hidden by a blind cap and depressed to fill a fountain pen

"Calligraph" popular model made by Mabie Todd with a special nib for calligraphy

capstan inkwell in the shape of a ship's capstan

case outer metal tube of a mechanical pencil

carrier tube brass tube running through the center of a mechanical pencil into which the propelling unit is fixed

coin filler pen with filling system in which a coin is pushed into a slot to depress the pressure bar on the sac

comb notched pattern on feed to store ink during writing

"combo" combination of a dip or fountain pen and a pencil in one unit

converter unit inserted into a pen to convert it from cartridge to ink fill

crescent filler pen with a curved metal unit protruding from the barrel, which depresses the sac for filling; invented and used mainly by Conklin

ding indentation in the metal cap or body

eraser term for a two-sided blade used for scraping parchment (i.e. to improve its ability to absorb ink)

eyedropper glass tube and rubber bulb used to fill pens; also refers to the pen itself

feed slotted unit in hard rubber or plastic, which fits into the section and supports the nib

ferrel metal tube at the end of a dip pen into which the steel nib fits

filigree decorative metalwork with cut-out designs

hatched engraved or indented with criss-cross patterns

hooded pen with only the tip of the nib showing

imprint engraving or stamp of the maker's name or logo

inner cap unit inside the cap to keep the pen sealed when not in use

insert simple glass or pot inkwell, which fits into an ornate holder

iridium hard metal used to make nib tips

lever mechanism for depressing a pressure bar onto the sac to fill a pen

lignum vitae very heavy hardwood from South America

morocco leather very thin leather used to cover items, including boxes and pen cases

manifold nib stiff, robust nib used for making copies and writing manifests

matchstick filler filling system with a small hole in the barrel into which a matchstick was pushed to depress the rubber sac

nozzle writing end of a mechanical pencil, supporting the "lead"

nib ejector sliding system to push out the nib on a dip pen

peg part of the section onto which the rubber sac is attached

pen writing instrument; synonymous in the 19thC with the nib

"Permanite" Parker's tradename for cellulose nitrate plastic

penner portable unit for carrying pens and ink

pierce hole hole in the nib that controls ink flow by allowing air back into the reservoir

piqué metal decoration, usually silver and gold inlaid into tortoishell

plunger small piston with a cork or leather seal or washer to aid ink fill

pressure bar metal bar inside the barrel, which compresses the rubber sac to expel air and allow the sac to fill with ink

propelling pin rod, which pushes "lead" out through the nozzle of the pencil

overlay metal laid over the barrel for decorative purposes

"Radite" Sheaffer's tradename for cellulose nitrate plastic

ring top pen with a ring attached to the cap for a chain or ribbon

repoussé relief decoration on metal produced by raising or beating from the back

repelling pencil pencil with "lead" that retracts mechanically

reservoir storage area in pens or pencils for ink or pencil "leads"

Rococo 18thC style typified by curves, scallops, shell shapes, and pastel colors

section unit, which holds the feed and nib, attached to the pen barrel

shell plastic cover for the nib, feed, and collector unit on a hooded pen

stanhope micro image fitted into a viewing hole behind a tiny lens

sac protector metal tube inside the barrel protecting the sac

snail design pattern in repoussé with swirls resembling a snail's shell

snorkel tube that extrudes through the section to draw up ink

stirrup stirrup-shaped loop or ring for mechanical pencils

telescopic extension mechanism, which pulls out like a telescope

"Vacumatic" Parker's process of evacuating air from the barrel of a pen to allow it to fill with ink

"wafer" thin slip of compressed adhesive used for sealing letters and other documents

waxjack 17thC unit featuring a roll of impregnated wick, used for melting sealing wax

Where to buy

New collectors are advised to buy from established auction houses, reputable dealers (preferably ones who come personally recommended), and vetted fairs such as those organized by collectors' clubs and societies (*see* pp. 62–3). A selection of addresses, including contacts for restoration, is listed below.

BRITISH AUCTION HOUSES

Bonhams (Knightsbridge)
Montpelier Street
London SW7 1HH

Phillips
101 New Bond Street
London W1Y 0AS

BRITISH DEALERS

ABC Lloyd
16 Stramongate
Kendal
Cumbria LA9 4BN

The Battersea Pen Home
PO Box 4161
London SW11 4XP

The Pen & Pencil Gallery
Church House
Skelton
Penrith
Cumbria CA11 9TE

The Pen Exchange
13 Chichester Rents
Chancery Lane
London WC2A 1EG

Penfriend
Bush House Arcade
Bush House
The Strand
London WC2B 4PH

Pens Plus
69–70 High Street
Oxford OX1 4BD

Portobello Road Antiques Market
Portobello Road
London W11
(Dealers include: Henry the Pen Man, John McKenzie, Sheila Steinberg, and Sue the Pen Lady)

Vintage Pencils
11–13 High Street
Harefield
Middlesex UB9 6BX

AMERICAN DEALERS

Berliner Pen
928 Broadway
Suite 805
New York NY 10010

The Fountain Pen Hospital of New York
10 Warren Street
New York NY 10007

Gary and Myrna Lehrer
16 Mulberry Road
Woodbridge CT 06525-1717

Pen Haven
3730 Howard Avenue
Kensington
Maryland 20893

Pendemonium
15231 Larkspur Lane
Montclair
Virginia 22026

BRITISH FAIRS

The London Pen Show
Contact Bonhams or
The Batttersea Pen Home

The Northern Writing Equipment Show
Contact The Writing Equipment Society (see pp.62–3)

AMERICAN FAIRS

The Chicago Show
Contact M. Fultz
1150 N. State Street
Ste 300 Chicago

The Washington Pen Show
Contact Ben Johnson
www.penciltrail.com/penshow

RESTORATION & REPAIR

Classic Repairs
PO Box 254
St Alban's
Hertfordshire AL4 0ZH

Pen Connection
39 Friar Street
Worcester WR1 2NA

Penfriend London Ltd
10–13 Newbury Street
London EC1A 7HU

Trevor Russell
5 Stoneyford Terrace
Uttoxeter ST14 8BW

How to learn more

There is a wealth of information on pens and writing equipment in books, magazines, auction-house catalogs, and on the internet. Societies publish quality magazines and membership is a great idea or beginners, although the best way of learning quickly is probably to attend one of the many writing-equipment shows, fairs, or auctions (*see* pp.60–61). The short list below should start you off.

WEBSITES

The Battersea Pen Home
www.penhome.com

David Nishimura
www.vintagepens.com

The Pen & Pencil Gallery
www.penpencilgallery.com

Pendemonium
www.pendemonium.com

Penfriend
www.penfriend.co.uk

BRITISH SOCIETIES

The Writing Equipment Society
Contact
Dr Maureen Greenland
Cartledge Cottage
Cartledge Lane
Holmesfield
Derbyshire S18 5SB

AMERICAN SOCIETIES

Pen Collectors of America
Contact
Boris Rice
P.O. Box 821449
Houston
Texas TX77282-1449

The Society of Inkwell Collectors
5136 Thomas Avenue South
Minneapolis MN 55410

What to read

BOOKS

Badders, V. Collector's Guide to Inkwells, vols 1 & 2 (Penducah, 1995/8)

Courtier, S., Marshall J.M., and Marshall, J.K. A Beginner's Guide to Collecting Pencils (Penrith, 1998)

Crosby, D. Victorian Pencils: Tools to Jewels (West Chester, 1998)

Dubiel, F. Fountain Pens: The Complete Guide to Repair and Restoration (Falls River, 1994)

Erano, P. Collecting and Valuing Fountain Pens (Salt Lake City, 1995)

Finlay, M. Western Writing Implements in the Age of the Quill (Wetherby, 1990)

Fischler, G. and Schneider, S. The Illustrated Guide to Antique Writing Instruments (West Chester, 1997)

Lambrou, A. Fountain Pens of the World (London, 1995)

Petroski, H. The Pencil: A History (New York, 1990)

Rivera, B. and T. Inkstands & Inkwells (New York, 1973)

Roe, G. Writing Instruments: A Technical History and How They Work (Manchester, 1996)

Steinberg, J. Fountain Pens (London, 1994)

MAGAZINES

Journal of The Writing Equipment Society
Contact The Writing Equipment Society (see pp.60–61)

The Pen & Pencil Gallery Magazine
Church House
Skelton
Penrith
Cumbria CA11 9TE

Pen World
International World Publications
3946 Glade Valley
Kingswood
Texas 77339

Pennant
See Pen Collectors of America

Index

Acknowledgments

The author would like to thank the following for their help in the preparation of this book, for their comments, and for providing items for photography: Alan Lloyd, Arthur Twydle, Ian Dixon, Mr and Mrs Head, Roadside Antiques of Greystoke, Samantha Grose, F. Dubiel, Alan Wedgebury, Henry Simpole, Richard Bloomfield, and, for much typing and many suggestions, Jane Marshall.

All pictures copyright Octopus Publishing Group Ltd. All pictures photographed by Tim Ridley, courtesy of Jim Marshall, except:
2 Octopus Publishing Group Ltd/Stuart Chorley; **19c**, **28l**, **38r**, **39l**, **45bl** Octopus Publishing Group Ltd/Premier Photography. **Jacket photograph**: Octopus Publishing Group Ltd/Stuart Chorley.